THE CHICKEN
C·O·O·K·B·O·O·K
Exciting Ideas for Delicious Meals

Photography by Peter Barry
Designed by Richard Hawke and Claire Leighton
Edited by Jillian Stewart and Kate Cranshaw
Recipes by Judith Ferguson, Lalita Ahmed and
    Carolyn Garner

3446
This 1996 edition published and distributed in
The United States of America by
Sweetwater Press, P.O. Box 1855, Florence, AL 35631
© Colour Library Books, Godalming, Surrey
Printed and bound in Hong Kong
ISBN 1-85833-529-9

THE CHICKEN
C·O·O·K·B·O·O·K
Exciting Ideas for Delicious Meals

SWEETWATER PRESS

Contents

Introduction

Chicken is one of the most popular meats eaten today. This is due, to a certain extent, to the large numbers of people who are eating less red meat in an attempt to reduce their fat and cholesterol intakes. In addition to being perfect for both healthy and low-calorie diets, chicken has the added advantage of being quick and easy to cook, as well as lending itself to a whole variety of cooking methods and complementary ingredients.

When choosing a fresh chicken, look at the skin. It should be pale and moist-looking, and the breast meat should be plump. Make sure that the packaging is intact, so that the chicken hasn't been exposed to the air – this goes for frozen chicken as well. Fresh chicken should be removed from its packaging and kept, covered, for no more than three days in the refrigerator. Frozen chicken should be thoroughly defrosted before using, and then cooked immediately. All chicken should be cooked from room temperature, but that does not mean that it should be left standing in the warm for a long time. When stuffing a chicken, do not pack the cavity tightly. Hot air must be allowed to circulate round to ensure that it cooks thoroughly. Chicken should never be cooked from frozen or partially thawed, and never be eaten pink or bloody.

As chicken is so popular, it can be bought in many forms; whole, quartered, or in portions – with or without bones. Although buying portions is convenient for the cook, it is expensive. It is much cheaper to buy a whole chicken and joint it yourself. Whole birds can also be bought as free-range or corn-fed (with a yellow-tinted skin), and these have a very good flavor. Young chickens, known as Cornish game hens, are also readily available. Depending on their size, they will each feed one or two people and make a very neat and attractive dish. Whole birds can also be boned and stuffed for special occasions, or "spatchcocked," by splitting them in half lengthwise up the underside and then flattening them out on skewers. Boneless breast fillets are one of the most popular portions, simply because they are so convenient for slicing, grinding, and cutting into bite-sized pieces.

With such a choice of cuts and cooking methods it is little wonder so many recipes for chicken exist. This book contains a variety of delicious recipes suitable for all occasions, and includes recipes from around the world, as well as more familiar appetizers and entrées. So, whether you want a dish for a cold winter's day, a dinner party, a lunch, or a Chinese meal, you need look no further than the recipes in this book.

CHICKEN SATAY

This typical Indonesian dish is very spicy, and makes an excellent appetizer.

SERVES 4

2 tbsps soy sauce

2 tbsps sesame oil

2 tbsps lime juice

1 tsp ground cumin

1 tsp ground turmeric

2 tsps ground coriander

1 pound chicken breast, cut into 1-inch cubes

2 tbsps peanut oil

1 small onion, minced

1 tsp chili powder

½ cup crunchy peanut butter

1 tsp brown sugar

Lime wedges and coriander leaves, for garnish

1. Put the soy sauce, sesame oil, lime juice, cumin, turmeric, and coriander into a large bowl and mix well.

2. Add the cubed chicken to the soy sauce marinade and stir well to coat the meat evenly.

3. Cover with plastic wrap and refrigerate for at least 1 hour, but preferably overnight.

4. Drain the meat, reserving the marinade.

5. Thread the meat onto 4 large or 8 small kebob skewers and set aside.

6. Heat the peanut oil in a small saucepan and add the onion and chili powder. Cook gently until the onion is slightly softened.

7. Stir the reserved marinade into the oil-and-onion mixture, along with the peanut butter and brown sugar. Heat gently, stirring constantly, until all the ingredients are well blended.

8. If the sauce is too thick, stir in 2-4 tbsps boiling water.

9. Arrange the skewers of meat on a broiler pan and broil under moderate heat for 10-15 minutes. After the first 5 minutes of cooking, brush the skewered meat with a little of the peanut sauce to baste.

10. During the cooking time, turn the meat frequently to cook it on all sides and prevent it browning.

11. Garnish the satay with the lime and coriander leaves, and serve the remaining sauce separately.

TIME: Preparation takes about 25 minutes plus at least 1 hour marinating. Cooking takes about 15 minutes.

SERVING IDEAS: Serve with a mixed salad.

TERRINE OF SPINACH AND CHICKEN

*This superb terrine is ideal when you want to impress your guests
with a delicious appetizer.*

SERVES 6-8

8 ounces chicken breasts, skinned and
   boned
2 egg whites
1 cup fresh white bread crumbs
4 cups fresh spinach, washed
1 tbsp each of minced chervil, chives, and
   tarragon
Salt and freshly ground black pepper
1¼ cups heavy cream
4 tbsps finely chopped English walnuts
Pinch of nutmeg

1. Cut the chicken into small pieces.

2. Put the cut chicken, 1 egg white, and half
of the bread crumbs into a food processor.
Grind until well mixed.

3. Put the spinach into a large saucepan
and cover with a tight-fitting lid.

4. Cook the spinach for 3 minutes, or until
it has just wilted.

5. Remove the chicken mixture from the
food processor and rinse the bowl.

6. Put the spinach into the food processor
along with the herbs, the remaining egg
white, and bread crumbs. Blend until
smooth.

7. Season the chicken mixture with a little
salt and pepper, and add half of the cream.
Mix well to blend thoroughly.

8. Add the remaining cream to the spinach,
along with the walnuts and the nutmeg.
Beat this mixture well to blend thoroughly.

9. Line a one-pound loaf pan with
parchment paper and lightly oil.

10. Pour the chicken mixture into the pan
and spread evenly.

11. Carefully pour the spinach mixture over
the chicken mixture, and smooth the top
with a metal spatula.

12. Cover the pan with lightly oiled
aluminum foil and seal this tightly around
the edges.

13. Stand the pan in a roasting tray and
pour enough warm water into the tray to
come halfway up the sides of the loaf pan.

14. Cook the terrine in a preheated 325°F
oven for 1 hour, or until it is firm.

15. Put the terrine into the refrigerator and
chill for at least 12 hours.

16. Carefully lift the terrine out of the pan
and remove the paper. To serve, cut the
terrine into thin slices with a sharp knife.

TIME: Preparation takes 25 minutes, cooking takes 1 hour, refrigeration
takes 12 hours.

SERVING IDEAS: Serve slices of the terrine on individual serving dishes
garnished with a little green salad.

CHICKEN-STUFFED PEPPERS

This is a lighter stuffing than the usual meat-and-rice mixture.

SERVES 6

3 large green or red bell peppers
¼ butter or margarine
1 small onion, minced
1 stick celery, finely chopped
1 clove garlic, crushed
3 chicken breasts, skinned, boned, and
    diced
2 tsps chopped parsley
Salt and pepper
½ loaf of stale white bread, made into
    crumbs
1-2 eggs, beaten
6 tsps dry bread crumbs

1. Cut the peppers in half lengthwise and remove the cores and seeds. Leave the stems attached, if wished.

2. Melt the butter in a skillet and add the onion, celery, garlic, and chicken. Cook over moderate heat until the vegetables are softened and the chicken is cooked. Add the parsley. Season with salt and pepper.

3. Stir in the stale bread crumbs and add enough beaten egg to make the mixture hold together.

4. Spoon the filling into each pepper half, mounding the top slightly. Place the peppers in a baking dish that holds them closely together.

5. Pour enough water around the peppers to come about ½ inch up their sides. Cover, and bake in a pre-heated 350°F oven for about 45 minutes, or until the peppers are just tender.

6. Sprinkle each with the dry bread crumbs and place under a preheated broiler. Broil until golden-brown.

TIME: Preparation takes about 30 minutes and cooking takes about 45-50 minutes.

VARIATIONS: Use green onions in place of the small onion. Add chopped nuts or black olives to the filling, if wished.

SERVING IDEAS: Serve as a first course, either hot or cold, or as a light lunch or supper with a salad.

Paotzu Steamed Buns with Chicken, Cabbage, and Mushrooms

These steamed dumplings could be eaten as part of a Chinese Dim Sum meal.

MAKES about 16

3 cups self-rising flour

2 tsps salt

1 tsp fresh yeast or 1 envelope dried yeast

1 cup warm water

½ cup shredded cabbage

6 dried black Chinese mushrooms (shiitake or cloud ear) pre-soaked and sliced

2 tsps sesame oil

1 cup ground chicken

1 tbsp chopped fresh root ginger

1 tbsp soy sauce

1 tbsp oyster sauce

Black pepper

1. Place the flour and salt in a large bowl. Sprinkle the yeast over the warm water, stir and leave for 10 minutes or until foaming.

2. Make a well in the center of the flour, add the liquid and stir in well, gradually incorporating the flour. Cover with a damp cloth or plastic wrap and leave in a warm place for 2 hours or until doubled in volume.

3. Combine the shredded cabbage and mushrooms. Heat the oil in a wok and add the cabbage, mushrooms, and chicken. Stir-fry rapidly for a few minutes. Add the remaining ingredients, stir together and remove from the wok. Leave to cool.

4. Knead the dough for 2-3 minutes, then cut into about 16 pieces. Roll each piece out to a 4-inch circle and place about 2 teaspoons of filling in the center of each circle.

5. Draw up the edges of the dough over the filling and pinch together. Place pieces of oiled nonstick baking parchment over the pinched ends and turn the buns over so they stand on the paper.

6. Leave the buns to stand, covered with the damp cloth, for 15-20 minutes, then place in a steamer and steam rapidly for 10-15 minutes or until firm, springy, and well risen. Serve immediately.

TIME: Preparation takes about 40 minutes, plus 2 hours 20 minutes for rising. Cooking takes 10-15 minutes.

WATCHPOINT: When steaming the buns, leave enough space between them for expansion. If necessary, cook in batches.

PREPARATION: Soak the mushrooms for 20 minutes in boiling water. Discard tough stalks before using.

TACOS

Packaged taco shells make this famous Mexican snack easy to prepare, so spend the extra time on imaginative fillings.

MAKES 12

12 taco shells

Chicken Filling

3 tbsps butter or margarine
1 medium onion, chopped
1 small red bell pepper, chopped
2 tbsps flaked almonds
12 ounces chicken breasts, skinned and
    finely chopped
Salt and pepper
1 piece fresh ginger, peeled and chopped
6 tbsps milk
2 tsps cornstarch
⅔ cup sour cream

Toppings

Shredded lettuce
Grated cheese
Tomatoes, seeded and chopped
Chopped green onions
Avocado slices
Sour cream
Jalapeño peppers
Taco sauce

1. Melt 2 tablespoons of the butter or margarine in a medium saucepan and add the onion. Cook slowly until softened.

2. Add the red bell pepper and almonds, and cook slowly until the almonds are lightly browned. Stir often during cooking. Remove to a plate and set aside.

3. Melt the remaining butter in the same saucepan and cook the chicken for about 5 minutes, turning frequently. Season and return the onion mixture to the pan, along with the chopped ginger.

4. Blend the milk and cornstarch and stir into the chicken mixture. Bring to the boil and stir until very thick. Mix in the sour cream and cook gently to heat through. Do not boil.

5. Heat the taco shells on a cookie sheet in a preheated 350°F oven for 2-3 minutes. Place on the sheet with the open ends downward.

6. To fill, hold the shell in one hand and spoon in about 1 tablespoon of chicken filling.

7. Next, add a layer of shredded lettuce, followed by a layer of grated cheese. Add your choice of other toppings and finally spoon some taco sauce over the mixture.

TIME: Preparation takes about 30 minutes. Cooking takes about 15 minutes for the chicken filling and 2-3 minutes to heat the taco shells.

COOK'S TIP: Placing the taco shells on their open ends when reheating keeps them from closing up and makes filling easier.

SERVING IDEAS: For a buffet, place all the ingredients out separately for guests to help themselves and create their own combinations.

SZECHUAN BANG-BANG CHICKEN

Serve this dish as an appetizer. The diners should toss and mix the ingredients together themselves.

SERVES 4

2 chicken breasts
1 medium cucumber

Sauce
4 tbsps smooth peanut butter
2 tsps sesame oil
½ tsp sugar
¼ tsp salt
2 tsps broth
½ tsp chili sauce

1. Simmer the chicken in a pan of water for 30 minutes or until tender. Remove the chicken breasts and cut them into ½-inch-thick strips.

2. Thinly slice the cucumber. Spread the cucumber on a large serving platter and pile the shredded chicken on top.

3. Mix the peanut butter with the sesame oil, sugar, salt, and broth. Pour the sauce evenly over the chicken. Sprinkle the chili sauce evenly over the top.

TIME: Preparation takes about 15 minutes and cooking takes 30 minutes.

VARIATIONS: Use crunchy peanut butter or tahini in place of smooth peanut butter.

PREPARATION: The chicken is cooked if the juices run clear when a sharp knife or skewer is inserted into the thickest part of the meat.

CHICKEN SCALLOPS

There are a multitude of different methods of cooking chicken, and this one, although one of the simplest, is also one of the most delicious.

SERVES 4

4 chicken breasts, skinned and boned
1 egg
8 tbsps whole-wheat bread crumbs
1 tbsp chopped fresh sage
Salt and freshly ground black pepper
2 tbsps walnut oil
½ cup mayonnaise
⅔ cup plain yogurt
1 tsp grated fresh horseradish or daikon
2 tbsps chopped walnuts
Lemon slices and chopped walnuts to
    garnish

1. Pat the chicken breasts dry with kitchen paper.

2. Whisk the egg with a fork until it just begins to froth.

3. Carefully brush all surfaces of the chicken breasts with the egg.

4. Put the bread crumbs onto a shallow plate and mix in the chopped sage. Season with a little salt and freshly ground black pepper.

5. Place the chicken breasts, one at a time, onto the plate, and carefully press the crumb mixture over the surfaces of the chicken.

6. Put the oil into a large, shallow skillet, and gently fry the prepared chicken breasts on each side for 6-7 minutes until they are pale golden and tender. Set them aside, and keep warm.

7. Mix all the remaining ingredients except those for the garnish, in a small bowl, whisking well to blend the yogurt and mayonnaise evenly.

8. Place the cooked chicken breasts on a serving dish, and spoon a little of the sauce over them. Serve garnished with the lemon slices and additional chopped nuts.

TIME: Preparation takes about 20 minutes, cooking takes about 15 minutes.

VARIATIONS: Use almonds instead of walnuts in this recipe, and limes instead of lemons. Oranges and hazelnuts make another delicious variation.

SERVING IDEAS: Serve with lightly-cooked green beans and new potatoes, or rice.

SALADE BRESSE

As well as being famous for its cheese, Bresse, in Burgundy, is renowned for its special breed of chickens, reputed to be the best in France.

SERVES 4-6

1 head radicchio, leaves separated and washed

1 head romaine lettuce, washed

1 bunch lamb's lettuce or watercress, washed

4 chicken breasts, cooked, skinned, and thinly sliced

½ cup Bresse Bleu or other blue cheese, cut in small pieces

16 cornichons (small pickles), thinly sliced

8-10 cherry tomatoes, halved and cored

2 tbsps walnut halves

Dressing

2 tbsps vegetable and walnut oil mixed

2 tsps white wine vinegar

¾ cup crème frâiche

2 tsps chopped fresh tarragon

Salt and pepper

1. Tear the radicchio and romaine lettuce into bite-size pieces. Leave the lamb's lettuce in whole leaves. If using watercress, wash thoroughly, remove the thick stems and any yellow leaves.

2. Toss the leaves together and pile onto a salad plate.

3. Place the chicken, cheese, cornichons, tomatoes, and walnuts on top of the lettuce.

4. Mix the oils and vinegar together and whisk well to emulsify.

5. Fold in the crème frâiche and add the tarragon, salt, and pepper.

6. Sprinkle some of the dressing over the salad to serve and hand the rest of the dressing separately.

TIME: Preparation takes about 20 minutes.

VARIATIONS: Use goat's cheese instead of Bresse Bleu, and yogurt or sour cream in place of the crème frâiche.

PREPARATION: The dressing can be made in advance and kept refrigerated.

CHICKEN WITH BLUEBERRY SAUCE

The sharp tang of blueberries makes an ideal partner for chicken.

SERVES 4

---

4 chicken breasts, boned and skinned
3 tbsps sesame oil
1 cup fresh blueberries
Juice of 1 orange
⅔ cup red wine
Sugar to taste
Orange slices and fresh blueberries to
   garnish

---

1. Season the chicken breasts with a little salt. Heat the oil in a skillet.

2. Gently sauté the chicken breasts for 6-7 minutes on each side, or until they are golden-brown and tender.

3. Meanwhile, put the blueberries in a small pan, along with the orange juice and red wine. Bring to a boil, then cover and simmer gently until the blueberries are soft.

4. Blend the blueberries and juice using a liquidizer or food processor for 30 seconds.

5. Rub the blended purée through a fine nylon sieve using the back of a wooden spoon, pressing the fruit through to reserve all the juice and pulp but leaving the seeds and skins in the sieve.

6. Put the sieved purée into a small saucepan and heat gently, stirring constantly until the liquid has reduced and the sauce is thick and smooth. Add a little sugar if the sauce is too sour.

7. Arrange the chicken breasts on a serving dish, and spoon the sauce over it. Garnish with orange slices and fresh blueberries.

TIME: Preparation takes 15 minutes, cooking takes approximately 15 minutes.

PREPARATION: To test if the chicken breasts are cooked, insert a skewer into the thickest part, then press gently. If the juices run clear, the meat is cooked.

VARIATIONS: Use cranberries instead of blueberries in this recipe.

Peking Egg Chicken with Beansprouts, in Onion and Garlic Sauce

This exciting mixture results in a simply delicious dish.

SERVES 3

3 chicken breasts
Salt and pepper
2 eggs
2 cloves garlic
2 green onions
4 tbsps oil
⅔ cup fresh beansprouts
4 tbsps broth
Wine vinegar to taste

1. Cut each chicken breast crosswise into 1-inch slices. Rub with salt and pepper.

2. Beat eggs lightly, and add the chicken slices to the eggs.

3. Crush the garlic and cut the green onions into 1-inch pieces.

4. Heat the oil in the wok. Add the chicken pieces one by one, and reduce heat to low. Leave to sauté for 2-3 minutes.

5. Once the egg has set, sprinkle the chicken with garlic, green onion, and beansprouts.

6. Finally, add the broth and vinegar to taste. Simmer gently for 4 minutes.

7. Remove the chicken, cut each piece into small regular pieces, and serve on a heated platter. Pour the remaining sauce from the wok over the chicken.

TIME: Preparation takes 10 minutes, cooking takes about 10 minutes.

COOK'S TIP: Buy the beansprouts on the day you intend to use them as they deteriorate rapidly.

SERVING IDEAS: Serve with a chili dipping sauce and rice.

CHICKEN WITH WALNUTS AND CELERY

Oyster sauce lends a subtle, slightly salty taste to this Cantonese dish.

SERVES 4

8 ounces chicken meat, cut into 1-inch
   pieces
2 tsps soy sauce
2 tsps brandy
1 tsp cornstarch
Salt and pepper
2 tbsps oil
1 clove garlic
½ cup walnut halves
3 sticks celery, cut in diagonal slices
⅔ cup chicken broth
2 tsps oyster sauce

1. Combine the chicken with the soy sauce, brandy, cornstarch, salt and pepper.

2. Heat a wok and add the oil and garlic. Cook for about 1 minute to flavor the oil.

3. Remove the garlic and add the chicken in two batches. Stir-fry quickly to cook the chicken without allowing it to brown. Remove the chicken and add the walnuts to the wok. Cook for about 2 minutes, until the walnuts are slightly brown and crisp.

4. Add the celery to the wok and cook for about 1 minute. Add the broth and oyster sauce and bring to a boil. When boiling, return the chicken to the pan and stir to coat all the ingredients well. Serve immediately.

TIME: Preparation takes about 20 minutes, cooking takes about 8 minutes.

WATCHPOINT: Nuts can burn very easily. Stir them constantly for even browning.

VARIATIONS: Almonds or cashew nuts may be used instead of the walnuts. If the cashew nuts are already roasted, add them along with the celery.

FLAUTAS

*Traditionally, these are long, thin rolls of tortillas with savory fillings,
topped with sour cream.*

SERVES 6

---

8 ounces chicken, skinned, boned and
    ground or finely chopped
1 tbsp oil
1 small onion, minced
½ green bell pepper, finely chopped
½-1 chili, seeded and finely chopped
½ cup fresh or frozen sweetcorn
6 black olives, pitted and chopped
½ cup heavy cream
Salt
12 corn or flour tortillas
Sour cream, guacamole, and taco sauce for
    toppings

---

1. Use a food processor or meat grinder to
prepare the chicken, or chop by hand.

2. Heat the oil in a medium skillet and add
the chicken, onion, and green bell pepper.
Cook over a moderate heat, stirring
frequently to break up the pieces of
chicken.

3. When the chicken is cooked and the
vegetables are softened, add the chili, corn,
olives, cream, and salt. Bring to a boil over
a high heat and boil rapidly, stirring
continuously, to reduce and thicken the
cream.

4. Place 2 tortillas on a clean work surface,
overlapping them by about 2 inches. Spoon
some of the chicken mixture onto the
tortillas, roll up and secure with cocktail
sticks.

5. Fry the flautas in about ½ inch oil in a
large skillet. Do not allow the tortillas to get
very brown. Drain on kitchen paper.

6. Arrange flautas on serving plates and top
with sour cream, guacamole, and taco
sauce.

TIME: Preparation takes about 15 minutes and cooking takes about
15 minutes.

VARIATIONS: Use guacamole instead of heavy cream.

SERVING IDEAS: Flautas are often served with rice, refried beans, and a
salad.

Eggplant and Chicken Chili

This unusual dish is both delicious and filling.

SERVES 4

---

2 medium-sized eggplants
4 tbsps sesame oil
2 cloves garlic, crushed
4 green onions thinly sliced, diagonally
1 green chili, finely chopped
12 ounces chicken breast
4 tbsps light soy sauce
2 tbsps broth, or water
1 tbsp tomato paste
1 tsp cornstarch
Sugar to taste

---

1. Cut the eggplants into quarters lengthwise using a sharp knife. Slice the eggplant quarters into pieces approximately ½-inch thick.

2. Put the eggplant slices into a bowl and sprinkle liberally with salt. Stir well to coat evenly. Cover with plastic wrap and leave to stand for 30 minutes.

3. Rinse the eggplant slices very thoroughly under running water, then pat dry.

4. Heat half of the oil in a wok or large skillet, and gently cook the garlic until it is soft, but not colored.

5. Add the eggplant slices to the wok and cook, stirring frequently, for 3-4 minutes.

6. Stir the green onions together with the chili into the cooked eggplant, and cook for a further 1 minute. Remove from the pan, and set aside, keeping warm.

7. Cut the chicken breast into thin slices with a sharp knife.

8. Heat the remaining 2 tablespoons of oil in the wok, and fry the chicken slices for approximately 2 minutes, or until they have turned white and are thoroughly cooked.

9. Return the eggplant and green onions to the pan and cook, stirring continuously, for 2 minutes or until heated through completely.

10. Mix together the remaining ingredients and pour these over the chicken and eggplants in the wok, stirring constantly until the sauce has thickened and cleared. Serve immediately.

TIME: Preparation takes about 10 minutes plus 30 minutes marinating, cooking takes approximately 15 minutes.

COOK'S TIP: The vegetables can be prepared well in advance, but the eggplants should be removed from the salt after 30 minutes, or they will become too dehydrated.

VARIATIONS: Use zucchini in place of the eggplants, if wished.

CHICKEN WITH CLOUD EARS

Cloud ears is the delightful name for an edible tree fungus that is mushroom-like in taste and texture.

SERVES 6

12 cloud ears, wood ears, or other dried Chinese mushrooms, soaked in boiling water for 5 minutes
1 pound chicken breasts, boned and thinly sliced crosswise
1 egg white
2 tsps cornstarch
2 tsps white wine
2 tsps sesame oil
1¼ cups oil
1-inch piece fresh root ginger
1 clove garlic
1¼ cups chicken broth
1 tbsp cornstarch
3 tbsps light soy sauce
Pinch salt and pepper

1. Soak the mushrooms until they soften and swell. Remove all the skin and bone from the chicken and cut it into thin slices. Mix the chicken with the egg white, cornstarch, wine, and sesame oil.

2. Heat the wok for a few minutes and add the oil. Add the whole piece of ginger and whole garlic clove to the oil and cook about 1 minute. Remove them and reduce the heat.

3. Add about a quarter of the chicken at a time and stir-fry for about 1 minute. Remove, and continue cooking until all the chicken is fried. Remove all but about 2 tablespoons of the oil from the wok.

4. Drain the mushrooms and squeeze them to extract all the liquid. If using mushrooms with stems, remove the stems before slicing the caps thinly. Cut cloud ears or wood ears into smaller pieces. Add to the wok and cook for about 1 minute.

5. Add the broth and allow it to come almost to a boil. Mix together the cornstarch and soy sauce and add a tablespoon of the hot broth. Add the mixture to the wok, stirring constantly, and bring to a boil. Allow to boil for 1-2 minutes or until thickened. The sauce will clear when the cornstarch has cooked sufficiently.

6. Return the chicken to the wok and add salt and pepper. Stir thoroughly for about 1 minute and serve immediately.

TIME: Preparation takes about 25 minutes, cooking takes about 5 minutes.

VARIATIONS: Flat, cup, or button mushrooms may be used instead of the dried mushrooms. Eliminate the soaking and slice them thickly. Cook as for the dried variety. Two teaspoons bottled oyster sauce may be added with the broth.

SERVING SUGGESTION: Cloud ears and wood ears are available from oriental supermarkets and some delicatessens. Shiitake mushrooms are more readily available fresh or dried. Both keep a long time in their dried state.

Chicken, Ham, and Leek Pie

The addition of cream and egg yolks at the end of the cooking time makes this pie extra special.

SERVES 6-8

1 × 3-pound chicken
1 onion
1 bay leaf
Parsley stalks
Salt and black pepper
1 pound leeks
2 tbsps butter
½ cup chopped cooked ham
1 tbsp parsley
1¼ cups chicken broth
12-14 ounces puff dough
⅔ cup heavy cream
1 egg, lightly beaten for glazing

1. Put the cleaned chicken in a large saucepan together with the onion, bay leaf, parsley stalks, and salt and pepper. Cover with cold water and bring gently to the boil. Allow to simmer for about 45 minutes, until the chicken is tender. Leave it to cool in the pan.

2. Meanwhile, wash and trim the leeks, and cut into 1½-inch pieces. Melt the butter in a small pan and gently sauté the leeks for about 5 minutes. Remove from the heat.

3. Take the cooled chicken out of the pan, remove the skin, and strip off the flesh. Cut it into good-sized pieces.

4. Put the chicken, ham, leeks, and parsley into a large pie dish with plenty of seasoning. Add 1¼ cups of the cooking liquid from the chicken.

5. Roll out the dough slightly larger than the size of the pie dish. Use the trimmings to line the rim of the dish. Dampen them and put on the dough lid. Trim and seal the edges together firmly. Any surplus dough can be used to make decorative leaves. Cut a few slits in the dough to allow the steam to escape. Brush the dough well with beaten egg.

6. Bake in the center of a preheated 450°F oven for 15 minutes. Remove and glaze again with beaten egg. Reduce the oven temperature to 400°F. Return the pie to the oven for another 20 minutes.

7. When the crust is well risen and golden-brown, remove the pie from the oven. Carefully lift off a segment of pastry and pour in the cream, which has been gently warmed together with the remaining beaten egg.

TIME: Preparation takes about 45 minutes for the chicken, plus extra cooling time, and 20 minutes to prepare the pie. Cooking takes about 35 minutes.

SERVING IDEAS: Serve with creamed potatoes and a green vegetable.

CRUMB-FRIED CHICKEN

A southern specialty, this dish has a slightly misleading name since most of the "frying" takes place in the oven!

SERVES 4-6

1 × 3-pound chicken
1 cup dry bread crumbs
½ cup Parmesan cheese
¼ tsp ground ginger
2 eggs, mixed with a pinch of salt
3 tbsps oil
¼ cup butter or margarine
Lemons and parsley for garnish

1. Preheat the oven to 400°F. To joint the chicken, first cut off the legs, bending them outward to break the ball-and-socket joint. Cut in between the ball-and-socket joint to completely remove the legs.

2. Cut down the breastbone with sharp poultry shears to separate the two halves. Use the poultry shears to cut through the rib cage. Use the notch in the shears to separate the wing joints from the back.

3. Use a sharp knife to separate the drumstick from the thigh. Cut the breasts in half with poultry shears.

4. Mix the bread crumbs, Parmesan cheese, and ground ginger together. First dip the chicken into the egg and then coat with the crumbs.

5. Heat the oil in a large skillet and add the butter. When hot, place in the chicken, skin side down first. Cook both sides until golden-brown.

6. Transfer to a cookie sheet with a slotted spoon and place in the oven for 20-30 minutes, or until the juices run clear when the chicken is tested with the point of a knife. Serve garnished with small bunches of parsley and lemon wedges or slices.

TIME: Preparation takes about 30 minutes. If using chicken portions, allow about 15-20 minutes for preparation. Chicken will take about 10-15 minutes to brown and 20-30 minutes to finish cooking in the oven.

PREPARATION: Mix the crumbs, cheese, and ginger on a sheet of wax or parchment paper. Place the chicken on the crumbs and shake the paper from side to side to coat easily and completely.

VARIATIONS: If wished, omit the Parmesan cheese and ginger, and add extra bread crumbs, paprika, salt, pepper, and a pinch of thyme.

INDIAN CHICKEN

Marinating chicken with spices allows their full flavors to penetrate the meat.

SERVES 4-6

1 × 3-pound chicken, cut into 8 pieces
2½ cups plain yogurt
2 tsps ground coriander
2 tsps paprika
1 tsp ground turmeric
Juice of 1 lime
1 tbsp honey
½ clove garlic, crushed
1 small piece ginger, peeled and grated

1. Pierce the chicken all over with a fork or skewer.

2. Combine all the remaining ingredients and spread half the mixture over the chicken, rubbing in well.

3. Place the chicken in a shallow dish or a plastic bag and cover or tie it. Leave for at least 4 hours or overnight in the refrigerator.

4. Arrange the chicken, skin side down, under a moderate pre-heated broiler, and cook until lightly browned. Turn over and cook the second side until lightly browned. This should take about 30 minutes in all. Baste frequently with remaining marinade.

5. Reduce the broiler heat and cook for 15 minutes, turning and basting frequently, until the chicken is brown and the skin is crisp.

6. Alternatively, bake the chicken in a covered pan in the oven at 325°F for 45 minutes – 1 hour and broil it for the last 15 minutes for flavor and color.

7. Serve any remaining yogurt mixture separately as a sauce.

TIME: Preparation takes about 15 minutes and marinating takes at least 4 hours. Cooking takes about 45 minutes.

COOK'S TIP: The chicken can also be barbecued. Make sure the shelf is on the level furthest from the coals so that the chicken has time to cook without burning.

VARIATIONS: Use only chicken breasts for this dish.

CHICKEN LIVERS WITH PEPPERS

Chicken livers are often overlooked as a tasty and nutritious food.

SERVES 4

---

4 dried Chinese shiitake mushrooms
1 pound chicken livers
1 inch fresh root ginger
1 tbsp rice vinegar
2 tsps sugar
1 small leek
1 onion
1 green bell pepper
1 red bell pepper
3 tbsps vegetable oil
2 green onion (scallion) "brushes" to
    garnish

---

1. Soak mushrooms in hot water for 20 minutes.

2. Clean and trim chicken livers, and blanch in boiling water for 3 minutes. Drain and slice.

3. Peel and finely slice ginger. Mix the vinegar and sugar, add the ginger, and set aside.

4. Clean and trim the leek and cut into thin rings. Peel and slice the onion and cut into strips. Core and remove seeds from peppers, and cut into strips.

5. Drain the mushrooms, remove hard stalks, and cut caps into thin slices.

6. Heat a wok, add the oil, and, when hot, add the mushrooms, onion, leek, and peppers, and stir-fry for 5 minutes. Remove and set aside.

7. Add the liver and the ginger mixture. Stir-fry for a further 5 minutes, return vegetable mixture to wok, and heat through. Serve garnished with green onion (scallion) "brushes."

TIME: Preparation takes 25 minutes and cooking takes about 15 minutes.

PREPARATION: To make green onion (scallion) "brushes," trim and slice the onion lengthwise, keeping the root end intact. Put into iced water and refrigerate until curled.

BUYING GUIDE: Dried shiitake mushrooms are available from Oriental stores. Some supermarkets sell fresh shiitake mushrooms, which don't require any soaking.

CHICKEN AND VEGETABLE STEW

A combination of chicken, lima beans, peppers, and onions made into an aromatic stew.

SERVES 4-6

1 × 3-pound chicken, cut in 8 pieces
⅓ cup butter or margarine
3 tbsps flour
1 large red bell pepper, diced
1 large green bell pepper, diced
6 green onions, chopped
2 cups chicken broth
⅔ cup canned or fresh lima beans
1 tsp chopped thyme
Salt, pepper, and a pinch of nutmeg

1. To cut the chicken in 8 pieces, remove the legs first. Cut between the legs and the body of the chicken.

2. Bend the legs outward to break the joint and cut away from the body.

3. Cut the drumstick and thigh joints in half.

4. Cut down the breastbone with a sharp knife, and then use poultry shears to cut through the bone and ribcage to remove the breast joints from the back.

5. Cut both breast joints in half, leaving some white meat attached to the wing joint.

6. Heat the butter in a large skillet and, when foaming, add the chicken, skin side down. Brown on one side, turn over and brown the other side. Remove the chicken and add the flour to the pan. Cook to a pale straw color. Add the peppers and onions and cook briefly.

7. Gradually stir in the chicken broth and bring to a boil. Stir constantly until thickened. Add the chicken, lima beans, thyme, seasoning, and nutmeg. Cover the pan and cook about 25 minutes, or until the chicken is tender.

TIME: Preparation takes about 35 minutes and cooking takes about 40 minutes.

PREPARATION: For crisper vegetables, add them after the chicken and sauce have cooked for about 15 minutes.

BUYING GUIDE: Buying a whole chicken and jointing it yourself is cheaper than buying chicken joints.

CHICKEN WITH SAFFRON RICE AND PEAS

Saffron is frequently used in Spanish recipes. While it is expensive, it gives rice and sauces a lovely golden color and delicate flavor.

SERVES 4

2 tbsps oil

1 × 2–3-pound chicken, cut into 8 pieces, skinned if wished

Salt and pepper

1 small onion, minced

2 tsps paprika

1 clove garlic, crushed

8 tomatoes, skinned, seeded, and chopped

1¼ cups rice

3 cups boiling water

Large pinch saffron or ¼ tsp ground saffron

¾ cup frozen peas

2 tbsps chopped parsley

1. Heat the oil in a large skillet. Season the chicken with salt and pepper and place it in the hot oil, skin side down first. Cook over moderate heat, turning the chicken frequently to brown it lightly. Set the chicken aside.

2. Add the onions to the oil and cook slowly until softened but not colored.

3. Add the paprika and cook for about 2 minutes, stirring frequently until the paprika loses some of its red color. Add the garlic and the tomatoes.

4. Cook the mixture over high heat for about 5 minutes to evaporate the liquid from the tomatoes. The mixture should be of dropping consistency when done. Add the rice, water, and saffron and stir together.

5. Return the chicken to the casserole and bring to the boil over high heat. Reduce to simmering, cover tightly, and cook for about 20 minutes. Remove chicken and add the peas and parsley. Cook a further 5-10 minutes, or until rice is tender. Combine with the chicken to serve.

TIME: Preparation takes about 20-25 minutes and cooking takes about 25-35 minutes.

VARIATIONS: Use fresh peas, podded, in which case allow about 3 cups of peas in their pods. Cook fresh peas with the rice and chicken.

SERVING IDEAS: This is a very casual, peasant-type dish which is traditionally served in the casserole dish in which it was cooked.

STIR-FRIED GROUND CHICKEN ON CRISPY NOODLES

Deep-fried crispy noodles are teamed up with the distinctively Oriental flavor of ginger and chicken in this simple recipe.

SERVES 2-3

8 ounces chicken breast meat
2 slices cooked smoked ham
6 slices fresh root ginger
1 large onion
3 green onions (scallions)
3 tbsps oil
½ tsp salt
2 tbsps soy sauce
2 tbsps chicken broth
1 tbsp vinegar
1 tsp hot pepper sauce
1 tsp sugar
2 tsp cornstarch

Crispy Noodles
1 pound egg noodles
Oil for deep frying
Salt
Sesame seed oil

1. Cook the noodles in boiling, salted water for 12-14 minutes, stirring occasionally.

2. Meanwhile, grind the chicken. Finely shred the ham, ginger, and onion. Slice the green onion (scallions).

3. Heat the oil in a large skillet and add the onion, ham, and ginger. Stir-fry for 2 minutes.

4. Add the ground chicken. Sprinkle with the salt, soy sauce, and broth. Stir-fry for a further 5 minutes.

5. Add the vinegar, sherry, hot pepper sauce, sugar, green onions, and cornstarch blended with 2 tablespoons water. Cook over high heat for 2 minutes.

6. When the noodles are cooked, drain well and pat dry with kitchen paper.

7. Fry the noodles in hot oil for 2-3 minutes, until very crisp. Drain well and sprinkle with salt and sesame seed oil.

8. Serve the chicken on a heated platter with the crispy noodles.

TIME: Preparation takes about 20 minutes, cooking takes about 10 minutes for the chicken and 12-14 minutes for the noodles.

CHICKEN COBBLER

This dish, with its creamy sauce and tender, light topping, is warming winter fare.

SERVES 6

4 chicken joints (2 breasts and 2 legs)
1½ quarts water
1 bay leaf
4 whole peppercorns
2 carrots, peeled and diced
24 pearl onions, peeled
6 tbsps frozen sweetcorn
⅔ cup heavy cream
Salt

Cobbler Topping
3½ cups all-purpose flour
1½ tbsps double-action baking powder
Pinch salt
5 tbsps butter or margarine
1½ cups milk
1 egg, beaten with a pinch of salt

1. Place the chicken in a deep saucepan with the water, bay leaf, and peppercorns. Cover and bring to a boil. Reduce the heat and allow to simmer for 20-30 minutes, or until the chicken is tender. Remove the chicken from the pan and allow to cool. Skim and discard the fat from the surface of the cooking liquid.

2. Continue to simmer the broth until reduced by about half. Meanwhile, skin the chicken and remove the meat from the bones. Strain the broth and add the carrots and onions. Cook until tender and add the corn. Stir in the cream, the seasoning, and add the chicken. Pour into a warmed casserole or into individual baking dishes and keep hot.

3. To prepare the topping, sift the dry ingredients into a bowl or place them in a food processor and process once or twice to sift.

4. Rub in the butter or margarine until the mixture resembles bread crumbs. Stir in enough of the milk to allow the mixture to stick together. If using a food processor, trickle the milk in down the food tube and process in short bursts to avoid overmixing.

5. Turn out onto a floured surface and knead lightly. Roll out with a floured rolling pin until the dough is about ½-inch thick.

6. Cut the dough into rounds using a 2-inch cookie cutter to form the "cobbles." Place the rounds on top of the chicken mixture. Brush the surface of the cobbler with the egg and salt mixture and bake for 10-15 minutes in a pre-heated oven at 375°F. Serve immediately.

TIME: Preparation takes about 20-30 minutes for the chicken, about 20 minutes to prepare the sauce, and the cobbler takes about 10 minutes to prepare. Final cooking takes about 10-15 minutes.

PREPARATION: Once the topping has been prepared, it must be baked immediately or the baking powder will stop working and the cobbler topping will not rise.

SESAME FRIED CHICKEN

Sesame seeds add a great, nutty flavor to chicken.

SERVES 4

1 cup all-purpose flour

1 tsp salt

1 tsp pepper

2 tsps paprika

2 tbsps sesame seeds

1 pound chicken breasts, or 4 good-sized
   pieces

1 egg, beaten, with 1 tbsp water

3 tbsps olive oil

1. Sift flour onto a sheet of parchment paper and stir in salt, pepper, paprika, and sesame seeds.

2. Dip chicken breasts in the egg-and-water mixture, then coat well in seasoned flour.

3. Heat a wok or skillet, add oil and, when hot, fry the chicken breasts until golden-brown on both sides.

4. Reduce the heat, and cook gently for 10 minutes on each side.

TIME: Preparation takes 10 minutes and cooking takes about 25 minutes.

PREPARATION: Add a little cayenne pepper to the paprika to make a spicy coating.

SERVING IDEAS: Serve with rice or new potatoes and carrots.

LEMON CHICKEN

Chicken, lemon, and basil is an ideal flavor combination and one that is frequently used in Greek cookery.

SERVES 4-6

2 tbsps olive oil
2 tbsps butter or margarine
1 × 3-pound chicken, jointed
1 small onion, cut in thin strips
2 sticks celery, shredded
2 carrots, cut in julienne strips
1 tbsp chopped fresh basil
1 bay leaf
Grated rind and juice of 2 small lemons
⅔ cup water
Salt and pepper
Pinch sugar (optional)
Lemon slices for garnishing

1. Heat the oil in a large skillet. Add the butter or margarine and, when foaming, add the chicken, skin side down, in one layer. Brown and turn over. Brown the other side. Cook the chicken in two batches if necessary. Remove the chicken to a plate and set aside.

2. Add the vegetables and cook for 2-3 minutes over a moderate heat. Add the basil, bay leaf, lemon rind and juice, water, salt and pepper, and replace the chicken. Bring the mixture to a boil.

3. Cover the pan and reduce the heat. Allow to simmer about 35-45 minutes or until the chicken is tender and the juices run clear when the thighs are pierced with the point of a knife.

4. Remove the chicken and vegetables to a serving dish and discard the bay leaf. The sauce should be thick, so boil to reduce if necessary. If the sauce is too tart, add a pinch of sugar. Spoon the sauce over the chicken to serve, and garnish with the lemon slices.

TIME: Preparation takes about 30 minutes, cooking takes about 45-55 minutes total, including browning of chicken.

VARIATIONS: Use limes instead of lemons and oregano instead of basil.

SERVING IDEAS: In Greece, this dish is often served with pasta. Rice is also a good accompaniment, along with a green salad.

TOMATO AND BACON FRIED CHICKEN

This unusual version of fried chicken is cooked in a tomato sauce flavored with garlic, herbs, and wine.

SERVES 6

Flour for dredging
Salt and pepper
1 × 3-pound chicken, cut into portions
6 tbsps oil
5 tbsps butter or margarine
1 clove garlic, crushed
1 small onion, finely chopped
½ cup diced bacon
6 tomatoes, skinned and chopped
2 tsps fresh thyme or 1 tsp dried thyme
Salt and pepper
⅔ cup white wine
2 tbsps chopped parsley

1. Mix the flour with salt and pepper, and dredge the chicken lightly, shaking the pieces to remove any excess. Heat the oil in a large skillet and, when hot, add the butter.

2. Add the chicken drumstick and thigh pieces, skin side down, and allow to brown. Turn the pieces over and brown on the other side. Brown over moderately low heat so that the chicken cooks as well as browns. Push the chicken to one side of the skillet add the breast meat, and brown in the same way.

3. Add the garlic, onion, and bacon to the skillet, and reduce the heat. Cook slowly for about 10 minutes, or until the bacon browns slightly. Add the tomatoes and thyme, and reduce the heat. Cook until the chicken is just tender and the tomatoes are softened.

4. Using a slotted spoon, transfer the chicken and other ingredients to a serving dish and keep warm. Remove all but about 4 tablespoons of the fat from the pan and deglaze with the wine, scraping up the browned bits from the bottom. Bring to a boil and allow to reduce slightly. Pour this gravy over the chicken to serve, and sprinkle with chopped parsley.

TIME: Preparation takes about 25 minutes and cooking takes about 30-40 minutes.

PREPARATION: Brown the chicken slowly so that it cooks at the same time as it browns. This will cut down on the length of cooking time needed once all the ingredients are added.

SPICY SPANISH CHICKEN

Chili, coriander, and bright red tomatoes add a warm, Spanish flavor to broiled chicken.

SERVES 6

6 boned chicken breasts
Grated rind and juice of 1 lime
2 tbsps olive oil
Coarsely ground black pepper
6 tbsps whole-grain mustard
2 tsps paprika
4 ripe tomatoes, skinned, de-seeded, and
    quartered
2 shallots, chopped
1 clove garlic, crushed
½ jalapeño pepper or other chili, seeded
    and chopped
1 tsp wine vinegar
Pinch salt
2 tbsps chopped fresh coriander
Whole coriander leaves to garnish

1. Place the chicken breasts in a shallow dish with the rind and juice of the lime, the oil, pepper, mustard, and paprika. Marinate for about 1 hour, turning occasionally.

2. To skin the tomatoes easily, drop them into boiling water for about 5 seconds or less, depending on ripeness. Place immediately in cold water. Skins should come off easily.

3. Place the tomatoes, shallots, garlic, chili, vinegar, and salt in a food processor or blender, and process until coarsely chopped. Stir in the coriander by hand.

4. Place the chicken on a broiler pan, reserving the marinade. Cook the chicken, skin side uppermost, for about 7-10 minutes, depending on how close it is to the heat source. Baste frequently with the remaining marinade. Broil the other side in the same way. Sprinkle with salt after broiling.

5. Place the chicken on serving dishes and garnish with coriander leaves or sprigs. Serve with a spoonful of the tomato relish on one side.

TIME: Preparation takes about 1 hour including marinating, and cooking takes 14-20 minutes.

PREPARATION: The tomato relish can be prepared in advance and kept in the refrigerator.

WATCHPOINT: When preparing chilies, wear rubber gloves or at least be sure to wash hands thoroughly after handling them. Do not touch eyes or face before washing hands.

CHICKEN POLISH STYLE

Choose small, young chickens for a truly Polish-style dish. A dry white roll was originally used for stuffing, but bread crumbs are easier.

SERVES 4

2 × 2-pound chickens
1 tbsp butter or margarine
2 chicken livers
6 slices crustless bread, made into crumbs
2 tsps minced parsley
1 tsp chopped dill
1 egg
Salt and pepper
⅔ cup chicken broth

1. Remove the fat from just inside the cavities of the chickens and discard it. Melt the butter in a small skillet. Pick over the chicken livers and cut away any discolored parts. Add chicken livers to the butter and cook until just brown. Chop and set aside.

2. Combine the bread crumbs, herbs, egg, salt and pepper, and mix well. Mix in the chopped chicken livers.

3. Stuff the cavities of the chickens and sew up the openings. Tie the legs together.

4. Place the chickens in a roasting pan and spread the breasts and legs lightly with more butter. Pour the broth around the chickens and roast in a preheated 375°F oven for about 40-45 minutes. Baste frequently with the pan juices during roasting.

5. To check if the chickens are done, pierce the thickest part of the thigh with a skewer or small, sharp knife. If the juices run clear the chickens are ready. If the juices are pink, return to the oven for another 5-10 minutes.

6. When the chickens are done, remove them from the roasting pan, remove the string, and keep them warm. Skim any fat from the surface of the pan juices. If a lot of liquid has accumulated, pour into a small saucepan and reduce over high heat. Pour the juices over the chicken to serve.

TIME: Preparation takes about 20 minutes and cooking takes about 45 minutes.

SERVING IDEAS: Serve with a cucumber salad or a Polish-style lettuce salad and new potatoes tossed with butter and dill.

VARIATIONS: Chopped mushrooms or onions may be added to the stuffing, if wished.

CHICKEN, SAUSAGE, AND OKRA STEW

There is an exotic flavor to this economical chicken stew. The garlic sausage adds instant flavor.

SERVES 4-6

½ cup oil
1 × 3-pound chicken, cut into 6-8 pieces
1 cup flour
1 large onion, minced
1 large green bell pepper, roughly chopped
3 sticks celery, finely chopped
2 cloves garlic, crushed
8 ounces garlic sausage, diced
5 cups chicken broth
1 bay leaf
Dash Tabasco
Salt and pepper
1 cup fresh okra
Cooked rice to serve

---

1. Heat the oil in a large skillet and brown the chicken all over, 3-4 pieces at a time. Transfer the chicken to a plate and set it aside.

2. Reduce the heat under the pan and add the flour. Cook over a very low heat for about 30 minutes, stirring constantly until the flour turns a rich, dark brown. Take the pan off the heat occasionally, so that the flour does not burn.

3. Add the onion, green bell pepper, celery, garlic, and sausage to the pan and cook for about 5 minutes over very low heat, stirring continuously.

4. Slowly add the broth, stirring constantly, and bring to a boil. Add the bay leaf, a dash of Tabasco and seasoning. Return the chicken to the pan, cover and cook for about 30 minutes or until the chicken is tender.

5. Top and tail the okra and cut each into 2-3 pieces. If the okra are small, leave whole. Add to the chicken and cook for a further 10-15 minutes. Remove the bay leaf and serve over rice.

TIME: Preparation takes about 30 minutes and cooking takes about 1 hour 25 minutes.

COOK'S TIP: The oil-and-flour paste may be made ahead of time and kept in the refrigerator to use whenever needed. If the paste is cold, heat the liquid before adding.

FRIED CHICKEN

Fried Chicken is easy to make at home and it's much tastier than a takeout!

SERVES 4

2 eggs
3 pounds chicken portions
2 cups flour
1 tsp each salt, paprika, and sage
½ tsp black pepper
Pinch cayenne pepper (optional)
Oil for frying
Parsley or watercress to garnish

1. Beat the eggs in a large bowl and add the chicken one piece at a time, turning to coat.

2. Mix flour and seasonings in a large plastic bag.

3. Place the chicken in the bag one piece at a time, close bag tightly, and shake to coat. Alternatively, dip each chicken piece in a bowl of seasoned flour, shaking off the excess.

4. Heat about ½ inch of oil in a large skillet.

5. When the oil is hot, add the chicken, skin side down. Fry for about 12 minutes and then turn over. Fry a further 12 minutes or until the juices run clear.

6. Drain the chicken on paper towels and serve immediately. Garnish with parsley or watercress.

TIME: Preparation takes about 20 minutes and cooking takes about 24 minutes.

PREPARATION: The chicken should not be crowded in the skillet. If the pan is small, fry the chicken in several batches.

COOK'S TIP: When coating food for frying, be sure to coat it just before cooking. If left to stand, the coating can become soggy.

TANGERINE PEEL CHICKEN

An exotic mixture of flavors blends perfectly in this delicious chicken dish.

SERVES 2

1 pound boned chicken breast, cut into
    1-inch pieces

Seasoning
½ tsp salt
1½ tsps sugar
½ tsp monosodium glutamate (optional)
1 tsp dark soy sauce
2 tsps light soy sauce
1 tsp rice wine or dry sherry
2 tsps vinegar
1 tsp sesame oil
2 tsps cornstarch

Oil for deep frying
1-2 red or green chilies, chopped
½-inch fresh root ginger, peeled and finely
    chopped
2 inches dried tangerine peel, coarsely
    ground or crumbled
2 green onions, finely chopped

Sauce
½ tsp cornstarch
1-2 tbsps water or broth

1. Mix the chicken pieces with the seasoning ingredients and stir well. Leave to marinate for 10-15 minutes. Remove the chicken pieces and reserve the marinade.

2. Heat a wok and add the oil for deep frying. Heat to 350°F, add the chicken pieces, and fry for 4-5 minutes, until golden. Drain chicken on paper towels, and keep hot.

3. Allow the oil to cool then pour off, leaving 1 tbsp oil in the wok. Stir-fry the chilies, ginger, tangerine peel, and green onions for 2-3 minutes. When they begin to turn color add the chicken and stir-fry for 1 minute.

4. Mix the reserved marinade with the sauce ingredients and pour this over the chicken. Stir and cook for 2-3 minutes until the sauce thickens and the chicken is tender. Serve immediately.

TIME: Preparation takes 20 minutes, including marinating time; cooking takes 15-20 minutes.

PREPARATION: Cook the chicken in batches.

COOK'S TIP: Have all the ingredients ready prepared before starting to cook.

CHICKEN WITH BEANSPROUTS

In this authentic recipe, marinated chicken is stir-fried with beansprouts and served with a sauce based on the marinade.

SERVES 4

---

4 boneless chicken breasts, skinned
1 tbsp Chinese rice wine
2 tsps cornstarch
½ cup beansprouts
2 tbsps oil
2 green onions, finely sliced
1 tsp sugar
1¼ cups chicken broth
Salt and pepper

---

1. Cut the chicken into thin slices or strips.

2. Place the chicken on a plate and pour the Chinese rice wine over it.

3. Sprinkle with the cornstarch and stir together well. Leave to marinate for 30 minutes.

4. Blanch the beansprouts in boiling, lightly-salted water for 1 minute. Rinse under cold running water and set aside to drain.

5. Remove the chicken from the marinade with a slotted spoon. Heat the oil in a wok and stir-fry the green onions and the chicken for 2-3 minutes.

6. Add the drained beansprouts and the sugar. Add the marinade and the broth. Allow to heat through. Check the seasoning, adding salt and pepper to taste. Serve immediately.

TIME: Preparation takes about 20 minutes, marinating takes 30 minutes. Cooking takes approximately 8-10 minutes.

VARIATIONS: Use half a small ordinary onion if green onions are not available.

WATCHPOINT: As soon as you add the marinade to the wok, the mixture will thicken so have the stock ready to pour in immediately, and stir continuously until all the ingredients have been fully incorporated.

CHICKEN AND SAUSAGE RISOTTO

This is a one-pot meal you can cook on the stove top.

SERVES 4-6

3 pounds chicken portions, skinned, boned, and cut into cubes
3 tbsps butter or margarine
1 large onion, coarsely chopped
3 sticks celery, coarsely chopped
1 large green bell pepper, coarsely chopped
1 clove garlic, crushed
Salt and pepper
1 cup uncooked rice
1 × 14-ounce can tomatoes
6 ounces smoked sausage, cut into ½-inch dice
4 cups chicken broth
Minced parsley

1. Use the chicken skin and bones and the onion and celery trimmings to make the broth. Cover the ingredients with water, bring to a boil and then simmer slowly for 1 hour. Strain and reserve.

2. Melt the butter or margarine in a large saucepan and add the onion. Cook slowly to brown, and then add the celery, green pepper, and garlic and cook briefly.

3. Add the salt and pepper and the rice, stirring to mix well.

4. Add the chicken, tomatoes, sausage, and broth and mix well. Bring to a boil, then reduce the heat to simmering and cook for about 20-25 minutes, stirring occasionally, until the chicken is cooked and the rice is tender. The rice should have absorbed most of the liquid by the time it has cooked. Sprinkle with the minced parsley to serve.

TIME: Preparation takes about 1 hour and cooking takes about 30-35 minutes.

PREPARATION: Check the level of liquid occasionally as the rice is cooking, and add more water or broth as necessary. If there is a lot of liquid left and the rice is nearly cooked, uncover the pan and boil rapidly.

SERVING IDEAS: Add a green salad to make a complete meal.

CHICKEN IN HOT PEPPER SAUCE

Stir-fried chicken served with peppers in a hot sauce.

SERVES 4

4 boned chicken breasts, skinned
2 tbsps oil
1 tsp chopped garlic
1 green bell pepper, cut into thin strips
1 red bell pepper, cut into thin strips
1 tsp wine vinegar
1 tbsp light soy sauce
1 tsp sugar
1½ cups chicken broth
1 tbsp chili sauce
2 tsps cornstarch
Salt and pepper

1. Cut the chicken breasts crosswise into thin strips.

2. Heat the oil in a wok and stir-fry the garlic, chicken, and the green and red bell peppers for 3-4 minutes.

3. Pour off any excess oil and deglaze the wok with the vinegar. Stir in the soy sauce, sugar, and broth.

4. Gradually stir in the chili sauce, tasting after each addition. Season with a little salt and pepper to taste.

5. Blend the cornstarch with a little water and stir into the wok. Bring to a boil, then simmer for 2-3 minutes. Serve piping hot.

TIME: Preparation takes 10 minutes and cooking takes approximately 10 minutes.

COOK'S TIP: Have all your ingredients ready prepared and measured out before you start to cook.

SERVING IDEAS: Serve with boiled or egg fried rice, on its own or as part of a Chinese meal.

CHICKEN IN SWEET-AND-SOUR SAUCE

This is an Italian agrodolce recipe more unusual than the familiar Chinese sweet-and-sour sauce flavors.

SERVES 4–6

2½ pounds chicken joints
1 large onion, chopped
1 large carrot, chopped
5 tbsps maraschino
5 tbsps white wine vinegar
½ cup water
1 bay leaf
15 juniper berries
4 tbsps olive oil
Salt and pepper

1. Mix together the chopped onion, carrot, maraschino, vinegar, water, juniper berries, and bay leaf. Marinate the chicken joints in the mixture for 4-6 hours.

2. Remove the joints from the marinade and drain well, reserving the marinade. Sauté the chicken in the olive oil until golden.

3. Place the chicken in a shallow casserole, add the unstrained marinade, cover and cook at 350°F for a about 1 hour or until the chicken is tender. Place on a warmed serving platter and keep warm.

4. Remove the bay leaf and press the cooking juices through a sieve. Reheat gently and pour the juices over the chicken to serve.

TIME: Allow 4–6 hours for the chicken to marinate. Cooking takes about 1 hour.

SERVING IDEAS: Accompany with pasta and an Italian bread such as ciabatta.

CHICKEN WITH RED PEPPERS

Easy as this recipe is, it looks and tastes good enough for company.

SERVES 4

4 large red bell peppers
4 skinned and boned chicken breasts
1½ tbsps oil
Salt and pepper
1 clove garlic, finely chopped
3 tbsps white wine vinegar
2 green onions, finely chopped
Sage leaves for garnish

1. Cut the peppers in half and remove the stems, cores, and seeds. Flatten the peppers with the palm of your hand and brush the skins lightly with oil.

2. Place the peppers skin side upward on the rack of a preheated broiler and cook about 2 inches away from the heat source until the skins are well blistered and charred.

3. Seal the peppers in a thick plastic bag and allow them to stand until cool. Peel off the skins with a small vegetable knife. Cut peppers into thin strips and set aside.

4. Place the chicken breasts between two sheets of dampened parchment paper and flatten by hitting with a rolling pin or steak hammer.

5. Heat the oil in a large skillet. Season the chicken breasts on both sides and add to the pan. Cook 5 minutes, turn over and cook until tender, lightly browned, and cooked through. Remove the chicken and keep it warm.

6. Add the pepper strips, garlic, vinegar, and green onions to the pan and cook briefly until the vinegar loses its strong aroma.

7. Place the chicken breasts on serving plates. Spoon the pan juices over them.

8. Arrange the pepper mixture over the chicken and garnish with the sage leaves.

TIME: Preparation takes about 35-40 minutes and cooking takes about 10 minutes to char the peppers and about 15 minutes to finish the dish.

VARIATIONS: For convenience, the dish may be prepared with canned pimiento instead of red bell peppers. These will be softer so cook the garlic, vinegar and onions to soften, and then add pimiento.

SERVING SUGGESTION: If fresh sage is unavailable substitute coriander or parsley leaves as a garnish.

CHICKEN AND PANCETTA ROLLS

These rolls can be prepared in advance and kept chilled until cooking time. They make perfect dinner party fare.

SERVES 4

4 large chicken breasts, skinned
⅓ cup butter, softened
1 clove garlic, crushed
1 tbsp fresh oregano leaves or 1 tsp dried
   oregano
Salt and pepper
16 slices pancetta or prosciutto ham

1. Place each chicken breast between two sheets of damp parchment paper and beat out each piece with a rolling pin or steak hammer to flatten.

2. Mix the butter, garlic, oregano, salt, and pepper together. Spread half of the mixture over each chicken scallop, then lay 4 slices of pancetta on top of each. Roll up, tucking in the sides, and secure with cocktail sticks. Spread the remaining butter on the outside of each roll.

3. Cook the rolls under a medium hot preheated broiler for about 15-20 minutes, turning occasionally, until tender. Slice each roll into ½-inch rounds to serve.

TIME: Preparation takes about 20 minutes and cooking takes 15-20 minutes.

VARIATIONS: The chicken rolls can be sautéed in a skillet.

SERVING IDEAS: Serve with a fresh tomato sauce, and accompany with rice or new potatoes, and green beans.

BLUE CHEESE CHICKEN

These chicken parcels make a lovely and unusual dish for a dinner party.

SERVES 4

---

4 ounces blue cheese

⅔ cup butter

2 tbsps heavy cream

1 tbsp parsley, finely minced

4 chicken breasts, skinned, boned, and
    beaten flat

8 slices bacon

2 tbsps oil

2 tbsps butter

⅔ cup dry white wine

⅔ cup chicken broth

Salt and pepper

2 tsps cornstarch

---

1. In a bowl, cream together the cheese and butter then add the cream to make a spreading consistency. Add the parsley.

2. Spread the cheese mixture on one side only of the chicken breasts, leaving a narrow border. Roll the breasts up, wrap each one in 2 bacon strips and secure with a cocktail stick or skewer.

3. In a flameproof casserole, heat the oil and butter together and, when sizzling, brown the chicken parcels on each side until golden.

4. Pour in the wine, chicken broth and seasoning (use very little salt because the cheese stuffing will be quite salty). Bring to a boil, cover, and simmer gently for about 40 minutes, turning occasionally.

5. When cooked, transfer the chicken to a hot serving dish and remove the sticks or skewers.

6. Blend the cornstarch in a cup with a little cold water and add to the pan juices. Stir until the sauce thickens; adjust seasoning if necessary, and pour the gravy over the chicken. Serve at once.

TIME: Preparation takes about 25 minutes and cooking takes 45-50 minutes.

PREPARATION: The chicken parcels can be prepared in advance of cooking and refrigerated until required.

SERVING IDEAS: Serve with rice or new potatoes and broccoli.

CHICKEN WITH OLIVES

This is a chicken sauté dish for olive-lovers. Use more or less of them as your own taste dictates.

SERVES 4-6

2 tbsps olive oil
2 tbsps butter or margarine
3 pounds chicken portions
1 clove garlic, crushed
⅔ cup white wine
⅔ cup chicken broth
Salt and pepper
4 zucchini, cut in ½-inch pieces
20 pitted black and green olives
2 tbsps minced parsley

1. Heat the oil in a large skillet and add the butter or margarine. When foaming, add the chicken, skin side down, in one layer. Brown one side of the chicken and turn over to brown the other side. Cook the chicken in two batches if necessary.

2. Turn the chicken skin side up and add the garlic, wine, broth, salt, and pepper. Bring to a boil, cover the pan, and allow to simmer over a gentle heat for about 30-35 minutes.

3. Add the zucchini and cook for 10 minutes. Once the chicken and zucchini are done, add the olives and cook to heat through. Add the parsley and remove to a dish to serve.

TIME: Preparation takes about 25 minutes, cooking takes about 50-55 minutes.

SERVING IDEAS: Serve with rice or pasta and tomato salad.

VARIATIONS: Artichoke hearts may be used in place of the zucchini.

POACHED CHICKEN WITH CREAM SAUCE

Poaching chicken keeps it tender and succulent.

SERVES 4

1 whole chicken (about 4½ pounds)
8-10 celery sticks, tops reserved
4 thick slices fat bacon
2 cloves garlic, crushed
1 large onion, stuck with 4 cloves
1 bay leaf
1 sprig fresh thyme
Salt and pepper
Water to cover
⅓ cup butter or margarine
6 tbsps all-purpose flour
1¼ cups light cream

1. Remove the fat from just inside the cavity of the chicken. Singe any pin feathers over a naked flame or pull them out with tweezers.

2. Tie the chicken legs together and tuck the wing tips under the body to hold the neck flap. Place the chicken in a large casserole or Dutch oven. Chop the celery tops and add to the pot. Place the bacon over the chicken and add the garlic, onion with the cloves, bay leaf, sprig of thyme, salt, pepper, and water to cover.

3. Bring to the boil, reduce the heat and simmer gently, covered, for 50 minutes or until the chicken is just tender.

4. Cut the celery into 3-inch lengths and add to the chicken. Simmer a further 20 minutes, or until the celery is just tender.

5. Remove the chicken to a serving place and keep warm. Strain the broth and reserve the bacon and celery pieces. Skim fat off the top of the broth and add enough water to make up to 2½ cups, if necessary.

6. Melt 1 tablespoon of the butter or margarine in the casserole and sauté the bacon until just crisp. Drain on kitchen paper and roughly crumble.

7. Melt the rest of the butter in the casserole or pan and when foaming, remove from the heat. Stir in the flour and gradually add the chicken broth. Add the cream and bring to the boil, stirring constantly. Simmer until the mixture is thickened.

8. Untie the legs and trim the leg ends. If wished, remove the skin from the chicken and coat with the sauce. Garnish with the bacon and the reserved celery pieces.

TIME: Preparation takes about 10 minutes and cooking takes about 1½ hours.

SERVING IDEAS: The chicken may be jointed into 8 serving pieces before coating with sauce, if wished. Cut the leg joints in two, dividing the thigh and the drumstick. Cut the breast in two, leaving some white meat attached to the wings. Cut through any bones with scissors.

CHICKEN WITH MANGO

The exotic flavors of mango and spices make a lovely combination in this dish.

SERVES 4

2 tbsps oil
1 tsp grated ginger
½ tsp ground cinnamon
4 chicken breasts, shredded
4 green onions, sliced diagonally
1 tbsp light soy sauce
1 chicken soup cube
⅔ cup water
1 tsp sugar
Salt and pepper
2 ripe mangoes, peeled and sliced, or 1 can
    sliced mangoes, drained
2 tbsps sherry

1. Heat a wok and add the oil. Add the ginger and cinnamon, and sauté for 30 seconds.

2. Add the chicken and green onions, and stir-fry for 5 minutes.

3. Add the light soy sauce, crumbled soup cube, water, and sugar, and bring to a boil.

4. Add salt and pepper to taste, and simmer for 15 minutes.

5. Add the mangoes and sherry, and simmer, uncovered, until the sauce has reduced and thickened.

TIME: Preparation takes about 10 minutes and cooking takes about 30 minutes.

PREPARATION: To cut up a fresh mango, first remove the peel then cut off the two rounded sides either side of the large flat stone.

SERVING IDEAS: Serve with boiled rice and snow-peas.

POULET GRILLÉ AU CITRON VERT

Crisp chicken with a tang of limes makes an elegant yet quickly-made entrée. From the warm regions of southern France, this dish is perfect for a summer meal.

SERVES 4

2 × 2-pound chickens
1 tsp chopped fresh basil
6 tbsps olive oil
4 limes
Salt, pepper, and sugar

1. Remove the leg ends, neck, and wing tips from the chickens and discard them.

2. Split the chickens in half, cutting away the backbone completely and discarding it.

3. Loosen the ball-and-socket joint in the leg and flatten each half of the chickens by hitting them with the flat side of a cleaver.

4. Season the chickens on both sides with salt and pepper and sprinkle with the basil. Place the chickens in a shallow dish and pour 2 tbsps of olive oil over. Squeeze the juice from 2 of the limes over the chicken. Cover and leave to marinate in the refrigerator for 4 hours or overnight.

5. Heat the broiler to its highest setting and preheat the oven to 375°F. Remove the chicken from the marinade and place in the broiler pan. Cook one side until golden-brown and turn the pieces over. Sprinkle with 1 tbsp olive oil and brown the other side.

6. Place the chicken in a roasting pan, sprinkle with the remaining oil, and roast in the oven for about 25 minutes. Cut the peel from the remaining limes, removing all the white parts, and slice them thinly. When the chicken is cooked, place the lime slices on top, and sprinkle lightly with sugar. Place under the broiler for a few minutes to caramelize the sugar and cook the limes. Place the chickens in a serving dish and spoon any remaining marinade over them with the cooking juices. Serve immediately.

TIME: Preparation takes about 25 minutes, plus 4 hours marinating, cooking takes about 35 minutes.

WATCHPOINT: Sugar will burn and turn bitter quickly, so watch carefully while broiling.

VARIATIONS: If you can get limes fresh from the tree, use the lime leaves instead of basil, or use fresh lemons and lemon leaves.

CHICKEN AND AVOCADO SALAD

The creamy herb dressing complements this easy summer salad.

SERVES 4

8 anchovy fillets, soaked in milk, rinsed, and dried

1 green, onion, chopped

2 tbsps chopped fresh tarragon

3 tbsps chopped chives

4 tbsps minced parsley

⅔ cup mayonnaise

⅔ cup plain yogurt

2 tbsps tarragon vinegar

Pinch each sugar and cayenne pepper

1 large head lettuce

4 cups cooked chicken strips or cubes

1 avocado, peeled, and sliced or cubed, coated with 1 tbsp lemon juice

1. Combine all the ingredients, except the lettuce, chicken and avocado in a food processor. Blend the ingredients until smooth and well-mixed. Leave in the refrigerator at least 1 hour for the flavors to blend.

2. Shred the lettuce or tear into bite-size pieces and arrange on plates.

3. Top the lettuce with the cooked chicken cut into strips or cubes.

4. Spoon the dressing over the chicken and garnish the salad with the avocado. Serve any remaining dressing separately.

TIME: Preparation takes about 30 minutes plus 1 hour refrigeration for the dressing.

PREPARATION: Dressing may be prepared ahead of time and kept in the refrigerator for a day or two.

Poulet Fricassée

This is a white stew, enriched and thickened with an egg-and-cream mixture which is called a liaison.

SERVES 4

---

4 tbsps butter or margarine
1 × 3-pound chicken, quartered and
    skinned
2 tbsps flour
2½ cups chicken broth
Grated rind and juice of ½ lemon
1 bouquet garni (parsley, bay leaf, thyme)
12-16 pearl onions, peeled
3 cups button mushrooms, whole if small,
    quartered if large
2 egg yolks
6 tbsps heavy cream
3 tbsps milk (optional)
Salt and pepper
2 tbsps minced parsley and thyme
Lemon slices to garnish

---

1. Melt 3 tablespoons of the butter in a large skillet. Add the chicken in one layer and cook over gentle heat for about 5 minutes, or until the chicken is no longer pink. Do not allow the chicken to brown. If necessary, cook the chicken in two batches. When the chicken is sufficiently cooked, remove it from the pan and set aside.

2. Stir the flour into the butter remaining in the pan and cook over very low heat, stirring continuously for about 1 minute, or until pale straw in color. Remove the pan from the heat and gradually beat in the chicken broth. When blended smoothly, add lemon rind and juice, return the pan to the heat, and bring to a boil, whisking constantly. Reduce the heat and allow the sauce to simmer for 1 minute.

3. Return the chicken to the pan with any juices that have accumulated, and add the bouquet garni. The sauce should almost cover the chicken. If it does not, add more broth or water. Bring to a boil, cover the pan, and reduce the heat. Allow the chicken to simmer gently for 30 minutes.

4. Meanwhile, melt the remaining butter in a small skillet, add the onions, cover, and cook very gently for 10 minutes. Do not allow the onions to brown. Remove the onions from the pan with a slotted spoon and add to the chicken. Cook the mushrooms in the remaining butter for 2 minutes. Set the mushrooms aside and add them to the chicken 10 minutes before the end of cooking.

5. Test the chicken by piercing a thigh portion with a sharp knife. If the juices run clear, the chicken is cooked. Transfer chicken and vegetables to a serving plate and discard the bouquet garni. Skim and discard any fat from the sauce and boil rapidly to reduce by almost half.

6. Blend the egg yolks and cream together and whisk in several spoonfuls of the hot sauce. Return the egg yolk and cream mixture to the remaining sauce and cook gently for 2-3 minutes. Stir the sauce constantly and do not allow it to boil. If very thick, add milk. Adjust the seasoning and stir in the parsley and thyme. Place the chicken in a serving dish and spoon the sauce over it. Garnish with lemon slices.

PECAN CHICKEN

Pecans can be used in both sweet and savory dishes. Here, their rich, sweet taste complements a stuffing for chicken.

SERVES 4

4 boned chicken breasts
3 tbsps butter or margarine
1 small onion, minced
⅓ cup pork sausage meat
⅔ cup fresh bread crumbs
1 tsp chopped thyme
1 tsp minced parsley
1 small egg, lightly beaten
½ cup pecan halves
1¼ cups chicken broth
1 tbsp all-purpose flour
2 tbsps sherry
Salt and pepper
Chopped parsley or 1 bunch watercress to garnish

1. Cut a small pocket in the thick side of each chicken breast using a small knife.

2. Melt 1 tablespoon of the butter in a small saucepan and add the onion. Cook for a few minutes over gentle heat to soften. Add the sausage meat and turn up the heat to brown. Break up the sausage meat with a fork as it cooks.

3. Drain off any excess fat, and add the bread crumbs, herbs, and a pinch of salt and pepper. Allow to cool slightly and add enough egg to hold the mixture together. Chop the pecans, reserving 8 of them, and add to the stuffing.

4. Using a small teaspoon, fill the pocket in each chicken breast with some of the stuffing.

5. Melt another tablespoon of the butter in a casserole and add the chicken breasts, skin side downward. Brown over moderate heat and turn over. Brown the other side quickly to seal.

6. Add the broth, cover the casserole, and cook for about 25-30 minutes in a preheated 350°F oven until tender.

7. When the chicken is cooked, remove it to a serving platter to keep warm. Reserve the cooking liquid.

8. Melt the remaining butter in a small saucepan and stir in the flour. Cook to a pale straw color. Strain the cooking liquid over it and add the sherry. Bring to a boil and stir constantly until thickened. Add the reserved pecans and seasoning.

9. Spoon some of the sauce over the chicken. Garnish with chopped parsley or a bunch of watercress.

TIME: Preparation takes about 30 minutes and cooking takes about 40 minutes.

VARIATIONS: Almonds, butternuts, hicory nuts or macadamias can be used instead. Crush macadamias roughly for the garnish and brown lightly in the butter before adding flour for the sauce.

SERVING IDEAS: Serve with a rice or sauté potatoes.

Poulet Sauté Vallée d'Auge

This dish contains all the ingredients that Normandy is famous for – butter, cream, apples, and Calvados.

SERVES 4

4 tbsps butter or margarine

2 tbsps oil

1 × 3-pound chicken, cut into 8 portions

4 tbsps Calvados

6 tbsps chicken broth

2 apples, peeled, cored, and coarsely chopped

1 shallot, minced

2 sticks celery, finely chopped

½ tsp dried thyme, crumbled

2 egg yolks, lightly beaten

6 tbsps heavy cream

Salt and white pepper

Garnish

2 tbsps butter

2 apples, quartered, cored, and cut into cubes

Sugar

1 bunch watercress or small parsley sprigs

1. Heat half the butter and all of the oil in a large skillet over moderate heat. When the foam begins to subside, brown the chicken, a few pieces at a time, skin side downward, then turn it. When all the chicken is browned, pour off most of the fat from the pan and return the chicken to the pan.

2. Pour the Calvados into a small saucepan and warm over gentle heat. Ignite with a match and pour, while still flaming, over the chicken. Shake the skillet gently until the flames subside. If the Calvados should flare up, cover the pan immediately with the lid.

3. Remove the chicken from the pan and reserve it in a warm place. Pour the broth into the skillet and scrape any browned chicken juices from the bottom.

4. Melt the remaining butter in a small saucepan or skillet. Cook the chopped apples, shallot, celery, and the thyme for about 10 minutes or until soft but not browned.

5. Combine the apple mixture with the broth. Place the chicken in a Dutch oven or casserole and pour the sauce over it. Place on high heat. Bring to a boil, then reduce heat, cover the pan and simmer for 50 minutes.

6. When the chicken is cooked, beat the eggs and cream. With a whisk, gradually beat in some of the hot chicken cooking liquid. Pour the mixture back into a saucepan and cook over a low heat for 2-3 minutes, stirring constantly until the sauce thickens and coats the back of a spoon.

7. Season the sauce with salt and white pepper, and set aside.

8. To make the garnish, melt the butter in a small skillet and when foaming, add the apple. Toss over a high heat until beginning to soften. Sprinkle with sugar, and cook until the apple begins to caramelize.

9. To serve, coat the chicken with the sauce and decorate with watercress or parsley. Spoon the caramelized apples over the chicken.

CORNISH GAME HENS WITH CHOCOLATE SAUCE

A small amount of unsweetened chocolate lends a rich depth of color and a delightfully mysterious flavor to a savory sauce.

SERVES 4

4 tbsps olive oil
4 single (small) Cornish game hens
Salt and pepper
3 tbsps flour
1 clove garlic, crushed
1¼ cups chicken broth
4 tbsps dry white wine
2 tsps unsweetened chocolate, grated
Lemon slices to garnish

1. Heat the oil in a heavy-based pan or casserole. Season the Cornish hens and place them, breast side down first, in the hot oil. Cook until golden-brown on all sides, turning frequently.

2. Transfer the Cornish hens to a platter and add the flour to the casserole. Cook to a pale straw color.

3. Add the garlic and cook to soften. Add the broth gradually, stirring well. Add the wine and bring to a boil.

4. Reduce to a simmer, replace the Cornish hens, and cover the casserole. Cook for 20-30 minutes, or until the Cornish hens are tender.

5. Transfer the cooked Cornish hens to a serving dish and skim any fat from the surface of the sauce. Add the grated chocolate and cook, stirring quickly, over a low heat for 2-3 minutes. Pour some of the sauce over the Cornish hens and garnish with lemon slices. Serve the rest of the sauce separately.

TIME: Preparation takes about 10 minutes, cooking takes about 35-45 minutes.

BUYING GUIDE: Unsweetened chocolate is not the same as plain chocolate, which must not be used as a substitute. It can often be found in Mexican stores.

SERVING IDEAS: Serve with rice and a vegetable such as peas or asparagus, or with a green salad.

TARRAGON CHICKEN PANCAKES

These attractive pancakes look sophisticated enough for a dinner party, but are so easy to make that you can indulge yourself at any time.

SERVES 4

1 cup whole-wheat flour
1 egg
1¼ cups milk
Oil for frying
3 tbsps butter
3 tbsps all-purpose flour
1¼ cups milk
Salt and black pepper, to taste
1 cup chopped, cooked chicken
1 avocado peeled, halved, pitted, and chopped
2 tsps lemon juice
1 tbsp chopped fresh tarragon

1. Put the whole-wheat flour into a large bowl, and make a slight well in the center. Break the egg into the well and begin to beat the egg carefully into the flour, incorporating only a little flour at a time.

2. Add the milk gradually to the egg-and-flour mixture, beating well between additions, until all the milk is incorporated and the mixture is smooth.

3. Heat a little oil in a small skillet, or crêpe pan, and cook about 2 tbsps of the mixture at a time, tipping and rotating the pan, so that it spreads evenly over the base to form a pancake. Flip the pancake over, to cook the other side.

4. Repeat this process until all the mixture has been used. Keep the pancakes warm, until required.

5. Melt the butter in a small saucepan, stir in the flour, and cook over a medium heat for 1-2 minutes. Remove from the heat and gradually stir in the milk. Bring to the boil, stirring, then simmer for 1-2 minutes. Season to taste.

6. Stir the chopped chicken, avocado, lemon juice, and tarragon into the sauce.

7. Fold each pancake in half, and then in half again, to form a triangle.

8. Carefully open part of the triangle out to form an envelope, and fill this with the chicken and avocado mixture.

TIME: Preparation takes about 25 minutes, and cooking takes about 25 minutes.

SERVING IDEAS: Serve piping hot, garnished with watercress and accompany with a crisp green salad.

CORNISH GAME HENS IN CURRY SAUCE

Whole roast Cornish game hens served with a spicy sauce make an interesting dinner party entrée.

SERVES 4

¼ cup butter
1 tsp oil
4 Cornish game hens
1 medium onion, finely chopped
1 clove garlic, crushed
2 tsps curry powder
⅔ cup chicken broth
Squeeze of lemon juice
2 tsps mango chutney
1 tbsp golden raisins
2 tsps cornstarch
Cold water

1. Put butter and the oil in a roasting pan and place in an oven preheated to 350°F. When sizzling, remove from the oven, add the Cornish game hens and baste well.

2. Return the pan to the oven and roast for about 35 minutes, basting at regular intervals until the hens are cooked. Test with a skewer inserted into the thickest part of the leg. If the liquid runs clear, the Cornish game hens are cooked. Remove from the roasting pan and keep them warm.

3. Drain off any excess fat from the pan and place it over a medium heat. Add the chopped onion and garlic, and sauté for a few minutes until softened. Reduce the heat, add the curry powder, and stir well for 2-3 minutes. Add the chicken broth and stir until it is bubbling. Add the squeeze of lemon juice, chutney, and golden raisins.

4. In a cup, blend the cornstarch with a little cold water and add it to the sauce. Mix well and cook for a few more minutes. Pour over the Cornish game hens or serve separately.

TIME: Preparation takes about 10 minutes and cooking takes about 40 minutes.

VARIATIONS: Substitute other sweet pickles for mango chutney for a different flavor.

SERVING IDEAS: Serve with Indian breads and rice.

Niçoise Chicken

The combination of fresh herbs, tomatoes, and black olives brings the taste of Provence to your table.

SERVES 4

4 boned chicken breasts, unskinned
4 tbsps oil
2 tbsps lemon juice

Tapenade filling

4 cups large black olives, pitted
2 tbsps capers
1 clove garlic, coarsely chopped
4 anchovy fillets
2 tbsps olive oil

Raw tomato sauce

4 cups ripe tomatoes, skinned, de-seeded, and chopped
1 shallot, very finely chopped
2 tbsps minced parsley
2 tbsps chopped basil
2 tbsps white wine vinegar
2 tbsps olive oil
1 tbsp sugar
Salt and pepper
1 tbsp tomato paste (optional)

1. Cut a pocket in the thickest side of the chicken breasts.

2. Combine half the olives, half the capers, and the remaining ingredients for the tapenade in a blender or food processor. Work to a purée.

3. Add the remaining olives and capers and process a few times to chop them coarsely.

4. Fill the chicken breasts with the tapenade. Chill to help filling to become firm.

5. Combine the oil and lemon juice and baste the skin side. Cook skin side down for 10 minutes under a pre-heated medium-hot broiler. Turn over, baste again, and broil for another 10 minutes on the other side or until tender.

6. Meanwhile, combine the tomato sauce ingredients, and mix very well. Serve with the chicken.

TIME: Preparation takes about 30 minutes and cooking takes about 20 minutes.

PREPARATION: Both the filling and sauce can be made in advance and kept refrigerated.

SERVING IDEAS: Serve with new potatoes and small green beans.

POUSSINS ESPAGNOLES

The olive oil in this recipe gives a wonderful flavor to the sauce.

SERVES 4

---

4 Cornish game hens
Salt and freshly ground black pepper
Olive oil, to brush
4 small wedges of lime or lemon
4 bay leaves
2 tbsps olive oil
1 small onion, thinly sliced
1 clove garlic, crushed
1 pound tomatoes
⅔ cup red wine
⅔ cup chicken or vegetable broth
1 tbsp tomato paste
1 green chili, seeded and thinly sliced
1 small red bell pepper, cut into thin strips
1 small green bell pepper, cut into thin
  strips
2 tbsps chopped, blanched almonds
1 tbsp pinenuts
12 small black olives, pitted
1 tbsp raisins

---

1. Rub the Cornish game hens inside and out with salt and pepper. Brush the skins with olive oil and push a wedge of lemon or lime, and a bay leaf into the cavity of each one.

2. Roast the Cornish game hens, uncovered, in a preheated 375°F oven for 45 minutes, or until just tender.

3. Meanwhile, heat the 2 tbsps olive oil in a large skillet and gently cook the onion and the garlic until they are soft, but not colored.

4. Cut a slit into the skins of each tomato and plunge into boiling water for 30 seconds.

5. Using a sharp knife, carefully peel away the skins from the blanched tomatoes.

6. Chop the tomatoes coarsely. Remove and discard the seeds and cores.

7. Add the chopped tomatoes to the cooked onion and garlic, and fry gently for a further 2 minutes.

8. Add all the remaining ingredients and simmer for 10-15 minutes, or until the tomatoes have completely softened, and the sauce has thickened slightly.

9. Arrange the Cornish game hens on a serving dish and spoon a little of the sauce over each one.

10. Serve hot and hand the remaining sauce in a gravy-boat.

TIME: Preparation takes 15 minutes, cooking takes about 45 minutes.

SERVING IDEAS: Serve with rice and a mixed green salad.

COOK'S TIP: If the Cornish game hens start to get too brown during the cooking time, cover them lightly with aluminum foil.

CHICKEN MARENGO

This classic dish uses expensive ingredients so save it for a special occasion.

SERVES 6

6 chicken portions
Salt and pepper
4 tbsps butter
¾ cup olive oil
4 ripe tomatoes, skinned and sieved
1 clove garlic, chopped
6 sprigs parsley (chop 5 sprigs)
2 cups dry white wine
8 ounces fresh wild ceps (boletus) or
    1½ ounces dried wild mushrooms
1 small white truffle or black truffle, sliced
1 small onion, diced
1 bay leaf
1 stick celery, chopped
Pinch of thyme
Peppercorns
6 uncooked jumbo shrimp
6 slices sandwich bread, crusts trimmed
6 eggs

1. Wash the chicken and pat dry with kitchen paper. Sprinkle with salt and pepper.

2. Heat 1 tablespoon of the butter and 6 tablespoons of the oil in a large skillet and brown the pieces of chicken, turning to cook evenly.

3. Add the tomatoes, garlic, and half the chopped parsley. Boil half of the wine for 2 minutes, add to the pan, cover, and cook over moderate heat for 20 minutes.

4. Meanwhile, trim the bottoms of the mushroom stems (if you are using fresh wild mushrooms), clean, and slice. If using dried mushrooms, soak for 30 minutes in warm water, then drain and chop.

5. Put 2 tablespoons of the butter in a pan with 2 tablespoons of the oil. Add the mushrooms and truffle slices to the pan. Sprinkle with salt and pepper and sauté until wilted. Before removing from the heat, sprinkle with the remaining chopped parsley.

6. Add the mushrooms to the chicken. Cover and simmer another 15-20 minutes or until the chicken is tender.

7. Meanwhile, heat the remaining wine in a saucepan. Add the onion, unchopped parsley sprig, bay leaf, celery, thyme, several peppercorns, and ½ teaspoon salt. When the wine comes to a boil, add the jumbo shrimp and simmer for 5 minutes; drain and reserve the shrimp, then shell and devein.

8. Heat the remaining oil in a skillet and fry bread slices until brown on both sides.

9. Heat the remaining butter in a large skillet and fry the eggs until the whites are firm and the yolks still soft. Remove from the heat and place the fried eggs on the slices of bread.

10. Place the chicken in the center of a large round serving platter. Spoon over the pan juices. Place the slices of bread with eggs around the edges, alternating with the jumbo shrimp.

TIME: Preparation takes 20 minutes, and cooking takes about 1 hour.

BUYING GUIDE: Dried ceps, or porcini to give them their Italian name, and jars of truffles are available from delicatessens and gourmet food stores.

CORNISH GAME HENS IN RED WINE

This dish, served with creamed potatoes and a green vegetable, is suitable for a winter dinner or dinner party.

SERVES 4

1½ tbsps oil
6 slices of fat bacon, chopped
2 medium onions, finely chopped
4 Cornish game hens
1¼ cups chicken broth
1¼ cups red wine
1 bay leaf
1 scant tsp thyme
1 cup mushrooms, thinly sliced

1. In a large casserole, heat the oil and sauté the bacon until crisp. Using a slotted spoon, remove the bacon to a plate. Add the onion to the oil and cook until soft. Remove.

2. Add the Cornish game hens to the oil, turning frequently, until the skin is slightly crisp. Add the chicken broth and red wine so that the liquid almost covers the birds.

3. Add the cooked bacon and onion, the bay leaf, thyme, and mushrooms and, placing the Cornish hens breast-side down, cook in an oven preheated to 350°F, for approximately 1½ hours. Test with a sharp knife. The meat should feel very tender. Remove the Cornish hens to a warm serving dish.

4. To the sauce add a beurre manié made from 2 teaspoons butter worked together on a plate with 2 teaspoons all-purpose flour. Add in small pieces, beating well with a wooden spoon. This will thicken the sauce, some of which can be poured over the Cornish hens. Serve the rest in a warm sauceboat.

TIME: Preparation takes 20 minutes and cooking takes 1 hour 35 minutes.

VARIATION: Use white wine for a change.

Index